The Next Level Of
Cryptocurrency Investing

Advanced Strategies For Building Wealth With Bitcoin
And Cryptocurrencies

Wayne Walker

Table of Contents

Cryptocurrencies

(besides Bitcoin): What Do They Do?

For the many people that are still in awe of the amazing price movements upwards that we have seen across a lot of the cryptocurrencies, the one question that I receive the most from new students and others is "what do they do?" Bitcoin of course gets the spotlight, but for the other cryptos most people draw a blank. Let us have a look at the more popular coins and later some thoughts on the market movements.

Ethereum (ETH) - Programmable contracts

Bitcoin (BTC) - Moving money, settling transactions, a digital asset

Dash (DASH) - Key feature is privacy

Monero (XMR) - Private digital cash

Litecoin (LTC) - Similar to Bitcoin but faster

Ripple (XRP) - Enterprise payment settlement network

NEO (NEO) - Ethereum for the Chinese market

Why Have They Appreciated So Much?

Besides the questions about what purpose do cryptocurrencies serve, the next hottest topic is about the market movements. The story that I share often in class is about when I traveled to New York City in May of 2017 on a working vacation. Then, Bitcoin was trading at a little over $2,200, I returned to Europe in August and it was over $4,000. Now what was fundamentally different about Bitcoin by August to warrant an almost doubling in price? On the surface not much, however, Bitcoin and cryptocurrencies in general, are based on trust in the systems that supports them. With that in mind, the rocketing of Bitcoin beyond $19,000 and altcoins making eye-popping gains, for anyone setting a limit on what "is reasonable" is clearly indulging in wishful thinking. There is no exact science or logic here.

How You Should Trade Them

From my background and training within the capital markets, forex specifically, many of the coins are in extreme overbought territory. From some of the reports that I have read from different analysts, Bitcoin will continue to make massive gains. I can't really laugh at them anymore or apply all of my previous training. What can be used, and I strongly suggest this for anyone trading any asset class is to "make failure survivable" not my quote, it is well known to engineers and people involved with startups. Invest or trade with risk capital across several of the coins that have sufficient volume so that your ability to enter and exit is relatively easy. I am aware there are many views on what is sufficient volume, I need to see at least a 1,000,000 plus. Finally, you can also consider cryptos as a hedge to your investments or trading. They qualify because as an asset class they do not correlate with other assets for example stocks or commodities. In the later chapters we will explore deeper into the best trading practices for crypto trading.

After All the hype

What Should You Really Have in Your Crypto Portfolio?

For even the casual observer the fall of 2017 into the first two quarters of 2018 have been a wild ride in cryptocurrencies. It appears for now, as I had written in articles on the web, some of the hype would subside and we can get on with real crypto trading and investing. Actually, a lot of what I wrote (less hype, more regulations) has come true.

It is not with an "I told you so" attitude that I write the hype is taking a vacation, I write because the hype needed a vacation for the long term good of cryptocurrencies. I am well aware many people have been burned and their accounts have taken a few knockout blows. To be honest some have given up on cryptos all together. The majority of the departing crypto traders are those who refused or neglected to get some training or qualified advice before diving in. I have stressed in my other books the importance of diversification. An important concept with all asset classes but with cryptos it goes from good to have to MUST HAVE. This diversification concept is nothing magical or some deep secret. Just having knowledge of basic trading principles along with technical analysis would have helped many with their strategy and especially their mind-set.

The Reality

The fact is that the volatility we have seen with Bitcoin has actually been more severe in the past. Cryptos like other markets can actually go down, this point seemed like a new idea to some. When we were having the run up with Bitcoin from $10,000 to over $19,000 faster than even the biggest fan could have imagined, the downside was forgotten. The reduction in hype has helped to mature the market and it has also forced traders to have a more strategic look at the sector. Another plus, the Bitcoin sell off has had the benefit of allowing several altcoins to step into the limelight, for example Stellar.

The Portfolio

What I would consider to include in a 2018 and beyond portfolio:

Bitcoin, Ethereum, Ripple, Cardano, Stellar, NEO, Litecoin, EOS, and Nem. They are selected from my principle that investors or traders should have a diverse portfolio of cryptos and only trade those with good liquidity (by crypto standards). All the selected are in the top 15 in terms of market capitalization.

Both the new and more experienced crypto enthusiast should be aware of the unique features of the individual coin. Each crypto asset has its distinct features in terms of market behavior. We have also seen that altcoins have their own price movement stories. It is not so simple to say, as was said in the past, that whatever Ethereum or Bitcoin does in the market the others coins will react with similar price movements. For example, the decline in Bitcoin did not lead to an equivalent drop for many altcoins. To the contrary, several have increased in value.

ICOs

Outside of my list of suggested coins there can also be room for the speculative ICO or two. This is considered with the knowledge that many, but NOT all, are scams. Once you have selected your cryptos, the next step to further diversify the portfolio is to ensure that you have the appropriate sector mix. The majority of investors miss this critical detail when assembling a portfolio.

Take Your Crypto Portfolio

Diversification to the Next Level

Serious investors are usually on board with the idea that diversity is desirable in a portfolio. Whether one is trading typically secure government bonds to volatile cryptocurrencies, diversity is one thing that we can all agree on. This is especially true when it is common knowledge that roughly a 1,000 persons own 40 percent of the Bitcoin market, the so-called "Bitcoin whales." The whales, by the way, are in other coins as well.

What I will do is expand on the concept and share more of the strategies that high-net-worth crypto investors use with their portfolios. As I have covered in some of my articles, you should aim to have a portfolio with a mix of cryptos to avoid the madness of having all your money in Bitcoin or Ethereum. To first step to noticeably increase your diversification is to diversify by sector, as in the feature, and or main purpose of the coin.

Crypto Diversity By Sector

Some of the sectors to begin with: Tokens, Conventional, Smart Contracts, Settlement Networks, Privacy, Overlay Service. The suggestions listed are just that, suggestions. This is obviously not a complete list of every coin from every sector. The list however is a good starting point when assembling your portfolio.

The sectors and possible coins

Token: Stratus, EOS

Smart Contracts: NEO, Ethereum, Cardano

Privacy: Monero, Dash, Zcoin

Conventional: Litecoin, IOTA, NEM

Settlement Networks: Stellar, Ripple

Crypto Diversity By Exchanges

Diversity of exchanges is often overlooked in the risk management process. This oversight was especially painful in 2017 when several of the most well-known exchanges in the East and West had issues dealing with the market rush. These issues took the form of: servers being overloaded, sites were down, and for many the most painful was being unable to remove profits. This is a 24/7 market and major moves can come at any time, therefore the ability to execute is paramount. You begin the process by carefully selecting according to a mix of factors including: if regulated or not, the country, speed of bank transfers, market reputation, etc.

Extending the Head Start

Just by incorporating the diversity of exchanges steps, you will have a clear head start on many investors. To extend your head start, the next step is to consider the weight of each sector or coin in your portfolio. For example, if you have 4 coins in a sector do they each get 25% allocation of your funds or if 4 sectors do they each receive 25%? The final composition takes into account many factors, for example, your risk tolerance, your exposure to other asset classes, and the size of your account. These are some of the things that I work on with clients to help them have a piece of mind.

You then continue the process by seeing what percentage of funds are with each exchange. The crypto market remains mostly unregulated, if your exchange goes bust there is very little help to get from any government, therefore being aware of what percentage of funds are sitting with each exchange is a necessary part of your risk management.

ICOs Overview:

The Good and What to Be Alert for

According to a recent survey, the majority of American adults did not know what an ICO was. An Initial Coin Offering (ICO) is similar to an Initial Public Offering (IPO). In an IPO investors are asked to purchase shares of a company in the company's bid to raise capital. However, with ICOs investors purchase the underlying crypto tokens in exchange for Bitcoin or Ether.

The first ICO was the Mastercoin Project in 2013 by J R Willet. It raised $500,000 in the form of 5,000 Bitcoins. Investors purchased Mastercoins in exchange for Bitcoins. The 5,000 Bitcoins that MasterCoin raised in 2013 was worth about $41 million in June 2018.

Hot and Risky

ICOs have been and remain a hot and risky sector of the crypto universe. As mentioned in the second chapter you do have to be careful with them. There have been comparisons to the dot-com bubble (1997-2001) but people should also keep in mind that the dot-com bubbles provided the opportunity for mega companies like Ebay and Google to expand.

Needed Answers

As an informed investor, you must review if the project really requires blockchain technology. Can the project of the ICO be done without it being a part of a blockchain? if so then this ICO might be just an attempt to get in on the ICO trend.

A few of the other questions that must be answered by any ICO: What is the point of the coin? What problem does it solve? Is it really a problem? You will also need to verify that the problem they plan to solve was not solved already by another coin. This is because when you read through some white papers you will quickly realize that you are dealing with a clone of another coin.

SPOTTING THE ICO SCAMMERS!

Some of the best warning signs that you are dealing with scammers

- Reaching them is difficult. The phone numbers they have can't be found by a simple web search
- The white paper is usually short (under 10 pages), filled with basic grammar or spelling errors
- The quality of the website is low or they used some free service to build it
- Their "about us" and registration details are questionable or missing
- The CEO or advisors can't be found on LinkedIn or other professional channels

Be Careful with Websites that Review ICOs

ICOs for the most part are unregulated which leads many people to ICO review sites to get a second opinion. Inexperienced investors are especially trusting of ICO rating platforms when seeking information. Rating platforms have always been suspect among experts because it is easy to buy ICO ratings. Basically, the ratings provided are not always independent.

"ICO ratings from the experts" is what some ICO rating platforms might advertise on their websites to gain the trust of investors looking for information. A nice claim, but investigations of the websites showed that ICO ratings and visibility are not always impartial. The results are frightening, you pay to play! Many platforms are nothing more than marketing sites selling to those willing to pay. They often offer priority listing services in exchange for payment. Bottom line, read the reviews with the knowledge that they may have been bought.

Traps To Avoid When Making the Transition

From Forex to Cryptocurrency Trading

How to transition successfully from forex to cryptocurrency is a challenge for many traders. Much of what I will share is based mostly on my experience with the transition to cryptocurrencies. Therefore, it is by no means the only way.

The first thing to be aware of is that a lot of what you know from trading spot forex can be applied to cryptocurrency, but there are some crucial differences. These differences, if ignored, can be fatal to your account.

The most important fact that forex traders must come to terms with is that they are not dealing with fiat currencies like the Euro or the US Dollar. Cryptocurrencies are not legal tender in any country, they are not currencies in the traditional sense. To put it another way, if you go to your local coffee shop they are not required to accept Bitcoin as payment. Now, if the coffee shop were in Madrid and you had Euros they would have to accept them because the Euro is legal tender in Spain. Cryptos are also subject to the regulatory whims of a government. A country, with little warning, could ban a crypto or a crypto exchange. This, on the other hand is not an everyday risk with fiat currencies. It is extremely unlikely that you will wake up tomorrow to a headline "US Dollar trading has been banned in the US" or "New York State has declared it illegal for residents to trade on NYSE."

The other issue that we are dealing with is technology. Cryptos can be programmed and I am unaware of any programmable fiats. We have also discovered with several of the cryptos that they have not been able to live up to their stated or promised capabilities. This doesn't even include the cases where there was outright fraud.

New Rules for News Trading

The normal strategies of foreign currency economic news trading do not directly apply. For example, a Non-Farm Payrolls jobs report or a Bank of England interest rate announcement will have little to no impact on Litecoin. However, your experience of dealing with reactions to news can be applied to cryptos, for example, a concept familiar to many forex traders is market overreaction to news. Overreaction to news is almost a cliché in cryptocurrency trading because most traders are both new and unfamiliar with market volatility. In addition, you have thought-paralyzing levels of madness that have me scratching my head when I hear the stories of people who have maxed out credit cards just to buy Bitcoins. If I were in a situation like that I guess I would be overreacting too.

Technical Analysis With 25,000% Returns

On the technical analysis front a lot of what you should already know about support and resistance is useful. What is new is that you will need to suspend strict interpretation of support/resistance levels. You have cryptos that can easily jump 100% per month and with many technical indicators this would be considered massively overbought, however, with cryptos a certain amount of suspension of disbelief is needed. Some proof, Pantera Bitcoin Fund returned over 25,000% (launched in 2013) or Ripple with 35,000% return for 2017. Not typos, both are easily verifiable with a simple Google search. The best way to deal with movements like these is to acknowledge that what is going on is not supposed to, but it is. As I have written before, we are in a new crypto universe that is expanding and changing with each day. Today what is legal can be suddenly illegal tomorrow. What you read and assumed to be true in the morning, can turn out to be "fake news" by lunch.

The whales of Bitcoin and cryptos in general are a real factor to deal with. As mentioned earlier they control more or less 40 percent of the market. This is unheard of in any other asset class. These whales depending on their mood can destroy your weeks of carefully planned analysis and strategy.

The entry of the institutional market players for example, Goldman Sachs and others will bring "smart" money to the market but especially liquidity. When they enter the market with huge amounts of capital this signals to other market players that cryptocurrencies are something to be taken seriously. Overall this is better for traders in general as it will help to mature the market along with the other mentioned benefits.

New York Stock Exchange (NYSE) has signaled in early 2018 that they are investigating the launch of a platform that will allow institutional clients to trade and store Bitcoins. This news alone could signal and form the basis of further price appreciation of Bitcoin and cryptos in general for the long term.

Death of the Purist

Being a fundamental or technical analysis purist will only leave you with an underperforming account. Therefore you will need a robust risk management strategy using many of the tools that should be familiar to you. You manage the risk by having as a foundation my non-negotiable rule of being able to survive failure, which means only trade what you can afford to lose. From there you add a diverse portfolio of cryptos and only trade those with good liquidity.

Crypto Exchanges:

Front-running and Pricing

Dealing with exchanges is a part of trading and with cryptos there are some issues that many investors are unaware of. The positive is that with the 24/7 market you can trade whenever it pleases you. The unpleasant reality is the front-running of your trades by the exchanges. Front-running is when a broker enters a trade ahead of its clients', usually done before a big trade that will likely influence the price of a crypto, stock, etc. This is both unethical and illegal in the regulated markets. Much of the crypto world is unregulated therefore exchanges have room to play. It is common knowledge that this practice is widespread in the market. For the most part, it is done with decent size trades because there is more of an incentive to profit from the front-running. If you are trading micro amounts of Bitcoin it really should not affect you.

Pricing and Spreads

The other hot topic with exchanges is pricing. Typically, on regulated exchanges, for example with stocks, you will usually get the best bid and ask prices. This is far more difficult to achieve with the crypto markets because the supply is so fragmented. The actual price that you will be executed on varies widely by the exchange that you use as a trading partner. One of the important variables includes how robust is the matching engine that they use. A trade matching engine is the software used by electronic exchanges, it matches up bids and offers to complete trades. Algorithms are used to execute the allocation. In addition to the two main issues that I covered, you could also run into latency problems if you are running an algorithm.

A spread is the difference between the buy and sell price. The spreads for cryptos when compared to other markets are huge. So huge that it was one of the hottest areas of complaints at the crypto trader event that I attended recently in New York City. As we have seen with other markets, the expectation is that the spreads will decrease with time.

None of this is meant to be an exchange bashing exercise, but instead an alert for traders. This is especially important for new traders and investors whom are often unaware of what they are dealing with when placing a trade. Exchanges do serve an important role in the market and remember that the cryptocurrency world remains relatively new and there is plenty of room to improve.

Security for
Your Account

With cryptos most of the responsibility for security rest with you, the individual user. If you choose to use an exchange they will play their role but in the end you are responsible. One of the reasons why security is such a big issue with blockchain transactions is that they are immutable and cannot be cancelled once done. For example, you send funds to another party by mistake, unless they feel like returning it, you should consider the funds lost. This is a benefit and risk of cryptocurrencies.

Why is There a Need for a Whole Chapter on Security?

Over $1billion has been stolen in cryptocurrencies within the past few years. The biggest theft was at Coincheck, 2018, with a loss of $500M, the well-known Mt. Gox 2014, had an estimated loss of $480M, and Parity Wallet 2017, an estimated loss of $155M. This is just a sample and I have only included _known_ thefts.

Some of the Common Attack Patterns

- Phishing: user details including 2FA (Two factor Authentication) are stolen on a fake site typically by email. The details are later entered into the real site after being captured from the fake one.

- Key logging viruses track user credentials when they log in and then compromises the account

- Copy and paste viruses hijack your paste function causing you to enter an attacker's address when transferring funds

- ICO sites have been copied and replaced by scammers, therefore be extra careful when participating in ICOs. Verify they are legitimate.

Medium to Advanced Security Practices

- Do not get phished. Never click a link and login from an email

- Do not use your regular email for your crypto trading account

- Always use Two factor Authentication for all

- Use different emails for each cryptocurrency exchange

- Use a trusted antivirus software and avoid questionable sites that may compromise your computer

- Remove the coins that you do not plan to trade in the short-term from the exchange

- Use a separate computer that is only used for crypto trading

- Keep as many coins as possible in a hardware wallet

- Wallets apps on your computer are good, but back up the private keys

Cryptojacking?

This is one of the newer forms of crypto misconduct. It involves the use of a computer to mine cryptocurrencies without the owner's permission. To be more direct, your computer is hijacked to work on someone's crypto mining.

The bad guys or girls execute the scheme by loading a program on your computer through the browser when visiting some compromised site. Shortly after, your machine begins solving computational problems that generate cryptocurrency mining rewards for the crypto-jackers. As you can imagine they will not share their rewards with you.

Your Defense

Keep a close eye on your computer's task manager. There are several browser extensions that will help your security efforts, one of them is MinerBlock from the Chrome web store. It blocks browser-based cryptocurrency miners.

The New World
of Government-Backed Cryptocurrencies

It did not take long for the cryptocurrency fever to begin infecting governments around the world. Several of them have recently announced their intentions to issue their own cryptocurrencies. This is an astonishing turnaround from those who on the surface might have an interest in stifling the spread of cryptocurrencies.

The Landscape

Venezuela has launched their cryptocurrency backed by the resources of the country, which mainly consists of oil and gas. It is called Petro and it mimics some of the features of Bitcoin. Venezuela, as many people know is suffering from a long list of economic ills. The American sanctions have not helped the situation and President Nicolás Maduro has made no attempt to conceal his goal that this Petro cryptocurrency will provide a new way of circumventing them.

Russia also announced their goal of introducing a crypto Ruble. The goal is similar to that of Venezuela, which is to navigate around current or future sanctions. Russia, however is not in the same economic emergency as Venezuela. From what I have researched and heard they have a more let us wait and see attitude, in contrast to Venezuela which has already launched.

Not to be left out, even the Bank of England (BOE) recently revealed they are exploring the option of their own BOE backed crypto. I can only imagine that many other central banks are also investigating the possibility of their own digital currencies.

The Reaction

The general attitude in the crypto universe and mine is that this journey forward has several ideological and practical barriers. The most obvious is that if these government cryptos are truly intended to replace Bitcoin or any cryptocurrency, they would contradict some of the most central features of the crypto world, which is having a permissionless and decentralized ledger. Permissionless is especially non-negotiable for cryptocurrency enthusiasts. This alone will have the sides clashing because one of the things governments find irresistible is the taste of control. In essence, with these state-backed cryptocurrencies they are playing digital dress up with their fiat currency. You don't like the Euro? No problem, we have it for you now in crypto format. They changed the name and packaging, but the DNA of government control remains. Many have mentioned another obvious, if the system gets hacked (we can pretty much guarantee there will be constant attempts) who covers the losses? Are governments ready to begin paying compensation once the Pandora's box of state-backed cryptocurrencies opens?

The Launch

Since the Petro coin 2018 second quarter release market players have had their eyes on Venezuela. The market reception so far has been mixed but it is still too early to pass a final verdict. The hackers I am sure were also eager for the launch. My advice to the Venezuelan government, if they are open to my suggestions, "make failure survivable." From a cryptocurrency purist point of view, any centralized cryptocurrency is playing dress up and a non-starter.

What to Expect with

Cryptocurrencies in the Near Future

These are purposely short-term expectations, because in my view, making long-term claims about cryptos is a fool's errand. We are in the very early stages in a shift from a total, once unquestioned, belief in government issued currencies into the potential that cryptocurrencies have to offer us. Just as with fiat currencies, belief and trust in the system in essential. The almost unbelievable gains that many of the cryptos have experienced is a mix of many factors including, news, speculators, and the value proposition of the individual coins. I would further claim that the increasing trust by the general public and the institutional finance sector is the major factor. For example, in 2017 the French firm Tobam launched the first Bitcoin mutual fund in Europe. Trust being what it is, it can change, therefore buckle up! Because for all the 900% plus gains, the market can easily produce just as dramatic drops if negative issues regarding trust reappear within the cryptocurrency ecosystem.

Less ICO Madness

The ICO madness will lose some of the irrational gold rush mentality and we will see improved self-policing from the current players in the market. We are already seeing a crackdown by regulators in the United States, Europe and elsewhere. The public and government regulators do have limits on what they will tolerate. We are also seeing more; search, identify, and prosecute missions from authorities globally on the ICO swindlers. This is great news for most people, the scammers are obviously unhappy.

More Regulations

I was recently made aware of the amount of agencies that claim jurisdiction over cryptocurrencies. This is just in the United States alone, you have the Treasury Department's FinCEN, the Securities and Exchange Commission, and the Internal Revenue Service. The story gets more bizarre, because there is not even agreement among the regulators on what Bitcoin is. For example, the IRS treats it as property and the Commodity Futures Trading Commission says it is a commodity. For market participants this bring confusion to new levels. Even with the confusion, to increase the trust of the broader retail and institutional markets, there is a need of more appropriate regulations for this growing market. This should also include swift and robust punishment for those engaging in misconduct.

With the regulations, you will often find there is a pattern that follows market innovations like cryptos. First, we have the Wild West, followed by overregulation to calm the public. Later the cooler heads prevail and there is a rollback of some rules and finally ending with a workable balance.

Expanded Practical Application of Cryptos

Myth number one and in my opinion the biggest about cryptos, is that they have no practical applications. The reality is that several of the major coins have real life applications and are related to improving existing sectors in the market. Legacy firms that push this "no practical applications" myth are rarely happy about innovations that did not come from themselves and are quick to discredit any challengers.

In January 2018 the money transfer firm MoneyGram agreed to test Ripple due to its speed with executing transactions. Ripple was designed to speed up money transfers and international transactions. It reduces both the money transfer time and costs. Since it was only a test we will need to wait for the final results but it clearly proves there are real-world applications.

Another example includes when Ethereum was used to execute a real estate transaction. It became news when the founder of TechCrunch used it and a smart contract* to buy an apartment in the Ukraine without the need of travelling to the country.

*Smart Contracts: can manage agreements between people, executing the terms of a contract when the mutually agreed upon terms and conditions are met.

Greater use of Cryptocurrencies in the Emerging Markets

We will likely see the continued spread of cryptocurrencies in the emerging markets. This is because cryptos are not controlled by any country or directly tied to any government's legal tender. The practical application of this means if a shaky government collapses, the value of a cryptocurrency like Bitcoin in most cases will be untouched. This benefit may seem unnecessary to your average developed western country, but in unstable countries the decentralization feature of cryptos has a *very* real and practical use.

Waiting to see more of

What I am eagerly awaiting to see more of in the near crypto future.

1-Exchanges will upgrade both security and their capacity to deal with demand surges. Even though crypto exchanges are not subjected to the same level of scrutiny as traditional exchanges, going forward this security issue will become increasingly difficult to keep talking around. Why? the crypto landscape has enough sad tales of hackings with millions being stolen. No region in the world gets to point fingers. It happens in the East and it also happens in the West, to both big and small exchanges. In contrast to funds in your local bank, if your account is hacked at an exchange, there is very little recourse to recovering your funds and as of this writing there is no insurance available. Everyone knows hackers are on a dedicated hunt after cryptocurrency accounts, therefore the defense needs to step up. The internal threats are another set of headaches, they range from insider trading to other financial misconduct from employees.

Several of the regulated and larger exchanges buckled under the demand for new accounts during the recent market explosions. They will get a pass this time around, but how many more times will the public or those in power remain so forgiving?

2- Autumn 2017 saw the launch of Bitcoin futures and it will be interesting to see how this plays out. The public has been asking for a more regulated market, well trading on a futures exchange is all about regulations. This was also the first time that Bitcoin traders could hedge their positions in a regulated market. They now have the ability to take the other side in the market by shorting.

3- More coins that eliminates the need for miners. Currently, the majority of Bitcoin mining is done by a handful of firms. Not a market healthy situation as they can use this influence in undesirable ways.

4- Improvements in the speed of Bitcoin transactions seems to be catching the attention of many industry influencers. Even for Bitcoin fans, the relatively slow pace of a routine transaction can be an issue. There are several cryptos that are taking on these challenges and I am excited to see how this develops.

Crypto Trader Zone

Introduction

This is content that deals specifically with cryptocurrency trading. It will be especially useful for those without a trading background. For those that are already trading it will provide some extra insights into the crypto market.

Bitcoin and Altcoin Trading

Cryptos provide volatility, as traders we love this, it is sweet music for us. Why? If you place a trade and nothing happens then you have just paid the spread to your broker for nothing. Trading is a business (or you should treat it as one), for you to recover your cost of the transaction (the spread) you need and want volatility.

Rumors and panics add to the volatility. There can also be extreme sensitivity to news, 20% daily moves are **not** uncommon. The autumn of 2017, even by crypto standards, the volatility that we saw was astonishing.

Advantages

There are usually no trade size minimums, in contrast to trading stocks, commodities, or spot forex. You can also short sell, therefore an up or a down market are both okay with you. Other advantages are that you have the ability to trade directly with the exchanges, brokers are not mandatory. You can trade 24/7 which is even more trading hours than spot forex. Obviously, the liquidity is not equal throughout the day, some times of the day are more liquid than others.

Day Trading

Day trade with caution! For now you are trading mostly against inexperienced traders, but the scene is changing. The autumn of 2017 saw the launch of Europe's first Bitcoin mutual fund in France. There are also reports of several hedge and private funds with huge resources prepping to enter the market.

Market Timing

Getting in at the "perfect time" with Bitcoin and cryptocurrencies is unrealistic. What is going on, weekly double digits gains, is not supposed to, but it is. Using strictly technical analysis or fundamentals will fail you. Look to buy on panic drops, bounces upwards after Bitcoin panic drops have been very profitable. One tactic to deal with the volatility is to have price alerts set for noticeable price moves. I strongly suggest that you accumulate gradually, cryptocurrency wealth takes time. Ignore, as much as possible, the Wild West hype going on. If your crypto position has a 100% + move up, take some profits. If you did not have an existing position, after a major breakout upwards, buy on the pullbacks. The best opportunities are there for the informed and less emotional. This is especially true in an arena with crypto traders who are untested with facing 40-50% drops.

Leverage

Leverage? Use with caution and only with entities that offer reliable stop losses. Bitcoin and cryptos in general, are assets that can move 20-30% (either direction) on some days, therefore your account can easily blow up. You lose money when you get taken out, and that can easily happen with high leverage. Bottom line, stay in the game and any long-term shorting is with extreme caution...keep in mind all the "deaths" of Bitcoin.

Before Investing in ICOs, Keep in Mind

Keep in mind with ICOs no one knows for sure which one will take off. If you invest in 5, there is a very good chance 3 to 4 will fail. But the one that does take off returns 10x or more. 10x means that if you invested $10mm, you generate $100mm in total when you sell.

A little tip: with ICOs or basic transactions, send fractions of payment to test transfers. Practice sending .001 for first few transactions, you can go out to 8 decimal places with Bitcoin.

You should be aware that many of the recent venture capital backed ventures have not brought their products to market as yet. In addition, the full uses of BTC and altcoins are just being explored. Many believe, with good reasons, that Bitcoin will be surpassed in value by another coin. Their basis is that rarely in technology does the first mover remain the dominant player after 5-10 years. Bottom line, we are in the early, early days of digital currencies.

Trading Tactics

Here we will examine the major reasons why traders lose money and most important we will explore the solutions.

Unrealistic Expectations: It is important when getting into trading, as with many things, that one must have a realistic idea of what you are dealing with. Unrealistic expectations can take the form of someone starting with what is a mini-trader account of 1,000 or maybe 2,000 USD and expecting overnight riches.

You can even begin with 100 or 200 dollars, which is fine. There is nothing wrong with the amount, but those same traders at 100 or 200 dollars are expecting to have 1,000 or 2,000 dollars in their accounts within a couple days. There are firms out there that have actually mentioned or even promised them that they can do this. While I am not saying it is impossible, I am saying it is unrealistic. It is essential that you do have a sense of reality to your trading.

No Plan: Many people say "failing to plan is planning to fail", with planning, your trading is in alignment with your timeframe and the results that you are expecting to receive. A trading plan is essential, because without one you are setting yourself up for potentially huge losses. Without a plan there is no point in entering trading.

Too Much Risk: It could be the person with 100 dollars in their account or even 100,000. It is not the amount that is critical, but the amount you are risking in relation to the funds available. You begin from the position of making "failure survivable". This concept is based on the idea that your losses should not be catastrophic. For example, each position should not use more than 5 or 6% of your available risk capital. This will also mean that if leverage is used it should be a low amount.

Confusing Trading With Investing: In my years as a banker, I have had countless clients who I have had to repeatedly point out that they should not confuse the two. Trading is about making money short-term, it is income generating activity, you are moving in and out of trades. Investing is more long-term and usually has a minimum timeframe of a year. It could be that some of your investment goals are derived from your trading but do not confuse them. It may seem basic to some, but speaking from experience of advising clients globally there are still many out there that get trading and investment confused.

Solutions:

It's ok to talk about problems and challenges, but obviously we need to have some solutions.

Low Leverage: To avoid the problem of too much risk, a proven solution is using low leverage. You keep the leverage low because it gives you time to think, to react more effectively, and you are not as sensitive to changes in the market.

Scaling In Scaling Out: Scaling in scaling out is one of my favorites. I use it with investing and also with my trading. Scaling in scaling out, the theory behind it is that you allow the market to tell you which way to go, it is that simple. An example, I plan to buy 250 of GCMS altcoins after having done my technical and fundamental analysis. How to begin? I would start with a 25 or 50 coins position and allow the market to confirm if I am on the right path. If I bought GCMS coins at 100 dollars and they suddenly jump to 125 per coin, great, the market is confirming that I made the correct decision. In this example if I began with 25 coins, I would then add another 25 or 50 and repeat the process until I reach my goal of 250 coins.

There are some who might say I missed out a little on the move from 100 to 125 and I did somewhat, but I am also more secure in my decision by being patient. On the reverse, getting back to scaling out, let us imagine that the market had moved against me, instead of having 250 coins at risk initially, it would have been only 25. Obviously there is a trade off, but from experience, it is to the advantage of those who are scaling in scaling out.

Another example, let us say you bought 100 coins at 100 dollars each and the price suddenly drops to 90. What I would suggest, instead of selling everything immediately, that you consider selling only 25 or 30 because the drop could be due to an overreaction in the market. There are several things that could be at play, for example a false rumor, again you are allowing the market to guide you along the correct path. Of course if the price continues to fall then you decide on a final exit if it goes beyond your mental stop loss.

Trade Liquid Markets: To trade liquid markets is something I can't overemphasize. Having one, long shot type trade (with ultra-risk capital) is fine, as long as you are aware of the risk. However, for regular trading, the cryptos with low liquidity by cryptocurrency standards, are not my first choice. Liquidity is critical especially as a trader, an investor is not as time sensitive, but if you are trading where you might need to make sudden moves you want to be holding liquid cryptocurrencies.

Liquid, to be very clear, is the ability to move in and out of the trade with ease. Being in a trade and having paper profits is wonderful. However, when it is time to convert the paper profits into real ones and if you are unable to do so, then it is a bad joke as you can only watch them, not very nice. On the other side if you are in a loss and are unable to exit that position, it turns into a nightmare. I don't care who is giving tips, or whatever blog you are reading, you must trade liquid cryptocurrencies, there is no other way.

Selecting Cryptocurrencies: Select a few and get to know them well. As you can imagine no trader is trading 600 different coins at a time. A lot of people begin with cryptos by trading the most well-known ones, Bitcoin, Ethereum, for example. After a while, by trading a few selected cryptos they will become familiar to you and you will get a deeper sense of how they move.

Putting It All Together

Traders must have a system. We will examine and connect the different aspects of a trading system.

Trading Platform: Selecting your trading platform is important because the platform is the vehicle that you use to conduct trading. Since the trading is online it is essential that you are using a platform that matches your style. It could be one that is either multi-asset or one that is more basic. You should know the provider behind the platform. With cryptocurrencies you have the option of using either a trading platform or dealing directly with an exchange. New exchanges are regularly popping up on the market and depending on the country you will need to be careful. I suggest that you get a recommendation from a friend or a trusted crypto advisor.

Goals: Without goals it is really difficult to begin trading. The analogy that I have heard and like to use, in regards to goals, is that without one it would be the equivalent of heading to a railway ticket counter and just say "give me a ticket!" and of course they would ask "a ticket to where?"
Short-term goals could be monthly or weekly profit targets, they are individualized. Goals must match your style and the amount of risk capital available for trading.

Long-term goals are often related to your investment strategy. They are also related to your short-term goals because the long-term goals should be based on the short-term profit targets. There must be a matchup, because if you have a weekly target of 100 dollars and a monthly target of a 1,000 then there is a discrepancy that needs to be addressed.

Mental Preparation: You do need to be psychologically ready to trade. If you are about to trade and are tense or nervous, then you need to take time off. Go meditate, get some exercise, do something else, but it is important that you do not trade until you are psychologically ready.

With trading you must have the mindset of not taking things personally. Remove emotions from trading, the goal is simply to make money.

Know your risk tolerance: How much are you willing to risk on each trade? It is important, remember traders' golden rule number one, "no cash, no trading." It doesn't matter what anyone tells you, if there is no cash, there is no trading and this must be taken seriously. This ties in with your risk tolerance, for example, having a cash balance of 10,000 USD and you want to risk 1%, the amount is 100 dollars. Meaning that of your risk capital, regardless of what you are trading, when you set your stop loss (mental or on a platform) it should not exceed 100 USD.

Do your due diligence: A new day has begun and your computer is on, what happened overnight? What happened on the crypto markets? You should be aware of the news that came out overnight and more importantly how the markets reacted to it. Sometimes, what in theory should be good news, the markets can surprise with a negative reaction.

How to select your entry level: Knowing your entry points means you have a good reason for every trade that you execute. If you do not have a good reason, I suggest that you take the funds and turn them over to a charity. When selecting your entry level, you need a good risk-reward ratio and this should match your risk tolerance. Technical/fundamental analysis is also taken into consideration. The support and resistance levels, news, are all essential before you execute any trade. If you are trading cryptos you need to be aware of where the support and resistance lines are for the time frame that you are trading.

Know Your Exit Levels: What is your profit target, is it a thousand dollars or a few? You need to be aware of this. When you are setting stops to control losses, the first thing to do is to ensure that they fall within your parameters. Same as with your entry level, you should know the fundamental analysis, support and resistance levels, and another traders' golden rule "cut your losses and let profits run." Many traders say the profits take care of themselves but you must keep a close eye on the losses.

Keep a Journal: It may not be for everyone but it is something that I use to record my trading. It includes several things, where I entered the trade, my exit level, and why I thought the trade was a good idea when I entered it. In review of your journal, if there are patterns, you will begin to detect them. You can either remove a pattern that is not working or expand on one that is. This helps you to fine-tune your trades.

Review Your Results: Review your profit or loss for the day. It is important because while trading can be fun, it is a business and the point is to make a profit. If in the review of your profit/loss you discover it is not what you had intended, your duty is to find out why. You also need to know what was behind your good results. Maybe it was pure luck, and if that was the case, great, but luck is normally not a sustainable strategy for trading. I would suggest, as I do in my trading, review your journal. Was it market news? Or was it the size of the positions? These factors can influence the results.

Crypto Technical Analysis Toolbox

The key point to making money with technical analysis is identifying the trend and trading along with it. Trends reveal to you where prices are most likely to head in the future. If the trend of a crypto is heading up, then you need to buy the crypto to make money. If the trend of a crypto is beginning to go lower, you need to sell the crypto to profit. If the trend of a crypto is sideways, with no clear direction, you either need to place contingent orders (not trades) or wait until a clear trend up or down is established before trading. It is not recommended to fight the trend, if you elect to do so, in most cases it will be an expensive experience for **you**.

Trends do not normally move straight up or straight down in a direct fashion. They usually move in one direction for a period of time and then temporarily retrace (reverse) part of the previous movement before continuing back on the original direction. Every time a crypto retraces and begins moving in the opposite direction, it forms a new high or a new low. For example, with cryptos, new highs form when a crypto moves higher and then turns around and moves lower. New lows form when a crypto moves lower and then turns around and moves higher. Identifying these highs and lows allows you to identify whether a crypto is in an uptrend, a downtrend or a sideways trend.

Uptrends - Markets that are trending upward form a series of higher highs and higher lows.

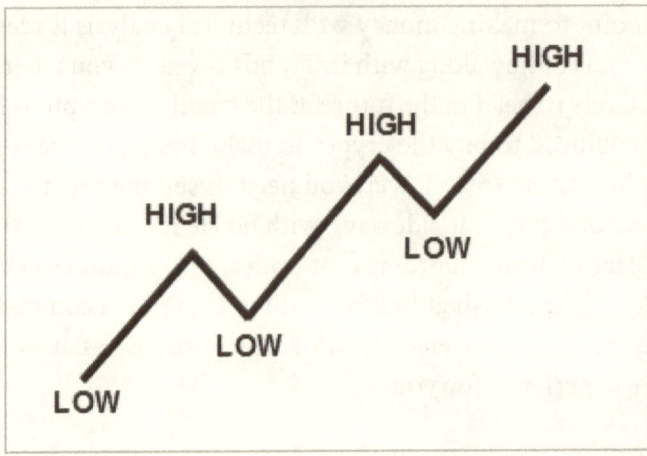

Downtrends - Markets that are trending downward form a series of lower highs and lower lows.

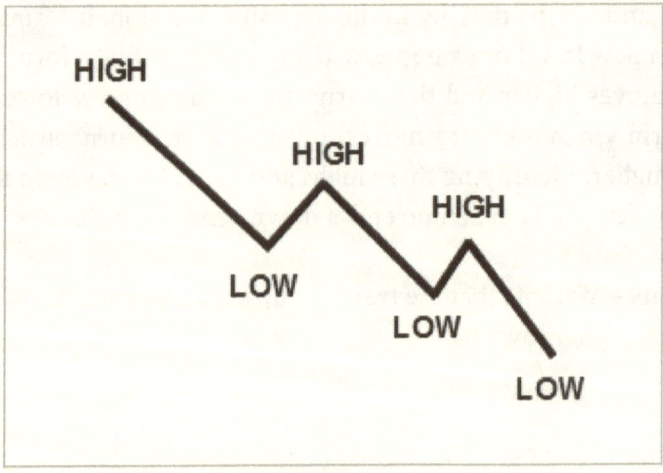

Sideways trends - A cryptocurrency that is trending sideways form a series of highs that are at approximately the same price level and a series of lows that are at approximately the same price level.

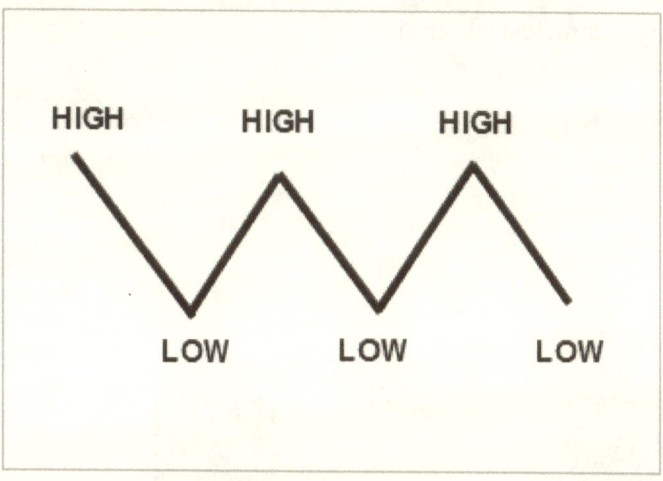

Trends - Whether they are uptrends, downtrends or sideways, trends can form over various time periods. Identifying the different trends over each timeframe and being able to align them in your analysis is crucial to your success as a trader.

Defining a candlestick chart

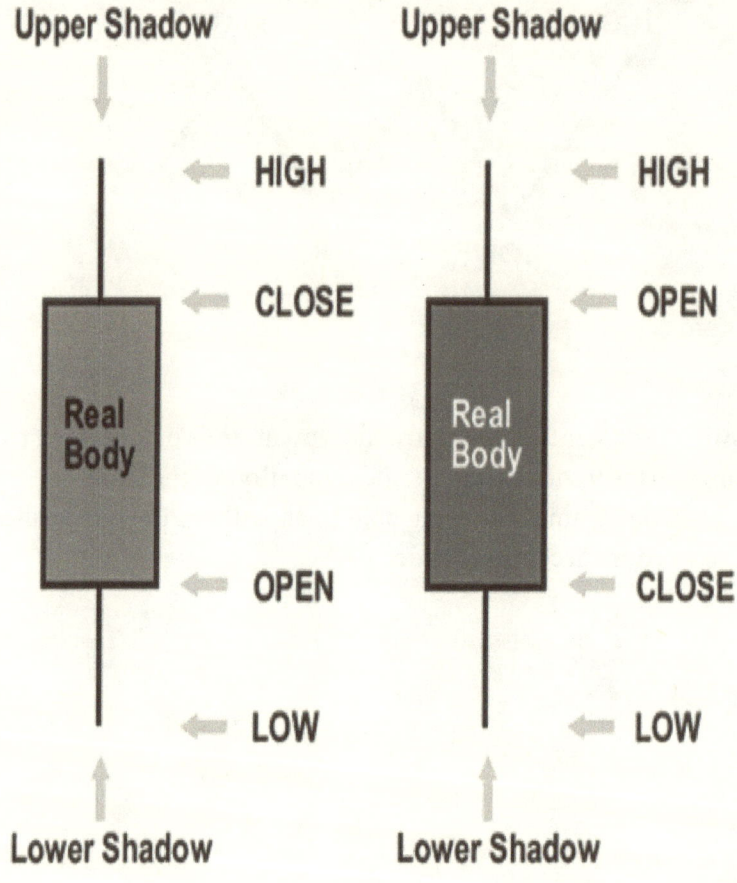

Let us begin by defining a candlestick. A candlestick is a line on a chart which represents one point and shows the high, low, open and close for each period. For example, if we have a daily chart, each candlestick represents one day and will show the high, low, open and close for that day. On many platforms, a red candlestick means that the close price is lower than the open price for that period. A green candlestick means that the close price is higher than the open price for that period.

Technical Analysis Indicators

We will take a look at the Moving Averages, RSI and Bollinger Bands indicators. First is the Moving Averages, and they are useful because they make it easier to spot a trend. This is key with currencies, cryptocurrencies or some of the derivatives where an up market is good and a down market is also good. Therefore, all we need to do is to identify or spot this trend. To illustrate, a fifty-day moving average adds up the closing prices for the last fifty days, divide by fifty and plots a point on the chart for each day.

Moving Average Chart

Let us review some basic settings with the moving average indicator. If we have settings on a chart of MA ten, MA fifty, then ten is the short-term, fifty is the long-term. The shorter moving average, if that is above the longer, the trend is considered upward. If the shorter moving average is below the longer moving average, then the trends is considered downward. On a chart if you see that the ten is breaking beneath the fifty, the long-term in this example, that could be taken as the initial sign of a sell signal.

With moving averages the buy and sell signals are generated by the price crossing above or below the moving average line. There is a term that you will hear a lot if you are around technical analysis folks, it is called the *golden cross* and it means that the short-term breaks above the long- term. The example we have is ten and fifty, but it could have been twenty and thirty, fifteen and seventeen, it depends on the trader and the instrument that they are trading.

Relative Strength Index

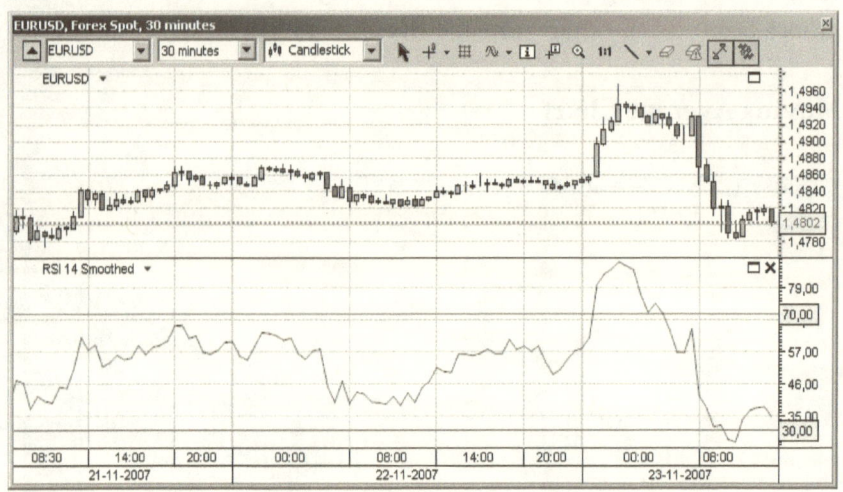

The RSI, which is the Relative Strength Index is used to identify if the market (stock, currency, cryptocurrency, etc.) is overbought or oversold. It is classified as a leading indicator because it begins giving signals before the trend has begun. It has an index from zero to one hundred.

The RSI graph is visible beneath the EURUSD chart. The RSI matches more or less what is happening on the chart and it should. Readings below thirty indicate that the market maybe oversold and when you see or hear the term oversold it mean excessive selling. Readings above seventy indicate that the market maybe overbought, excessive buying. Keep in mind these are indications, they are not guarantees of anything. As a note, the market can remain overbought or oversold for a considerable period of time.

Bollinger Bands

Bollinger Bands are a tool that many investors and traders use when they want to add different technical analysis aspects to the trades that they have open. They are used to measure market volatility. The bands define the upper and lower limits of the trading range. When you view the bands on a chart, you will have a top and a bottom band. The space between the top and the bottom, is called the buy - sell channel. You use the space between the bands to get an idea of where you are within the trading range. If you are near the top, you know that you are close to the resistance level and there is a potential for a price reversal (the market reverses direction). If you are at the bottom, you know that you are near the support level for a potential price reversal there. For the most part prices do remain between the bands. If the price begins to break out, many traders take this as a signal so you do need to be aware of that.

Understanding Support and Resistance Levels

Support level is the price level at which the instrument traded has historically had difficulty falling below. For example, if we have support around 1.4380, you would be able to see on a chart that the market has been to that level (1.4380) several times without falling lower, so in technical analysis jargon this would be considered a support level. Resistance level is just the opposite, the price level at which the instrument has historically had difficulty trading above.

Chart patterns similar to the letters M & W

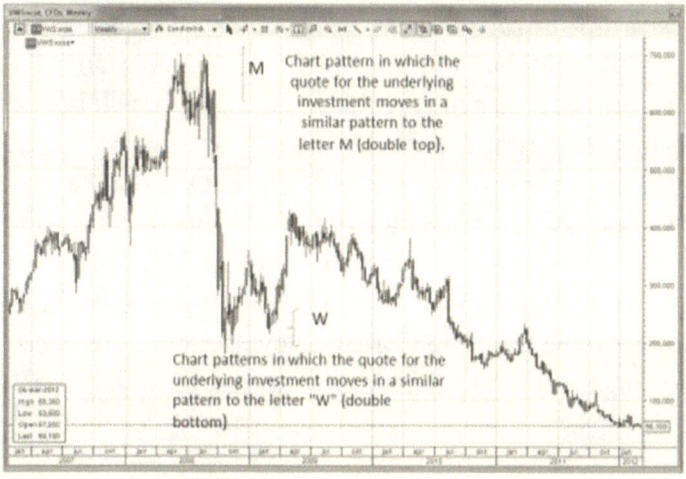

Chart pattern in which the quote for the underlying investment moves in a similar pattern to the letter M (double top).

Chart patterns in which the quote for the underlying investment moves in a similar pattern to the letter "W" (double bottom)

Chart Patterns "W" Double Bottom or "M" Double Top

These are chart patterns in which the price quoted for the instrument moves in a pattern similar to the letter "W" (double bottom) or "M" (double top). Double top and bottom patterns are used in technical analysis to explain movements in a stock, cryptocurrency or other investments, and can be used as part of a trading strategy to exploit recurring patterns. A double top and a double bottom are both trend reversal patterns.

A **double bottom** tends to occur after a strong downtrend, and it indicates that an uptrend may be imminent. The "bottoms" are valleys which are formed when the price hits a certain support level that cannot be broken. After hitting this level, the price will bounce off it slightly before returning to test the level again. If the price bounces off the support a second time, then you have a double bottom formation. If the second bottom cannot break the low of the first, then this is a strong signal that a reversal is going to happen. A ′neckline′ is drawn at the high between the two ′bottoms′. With a double bottom, you could think of placing your long (buy) entry order above the 'neckline' because you are expecting the trend to change upwards.

A **double top** is usually formed after an extended uptrend, and it indicates that a downtrend may be imminent. The "tops" are peaks which are formed when the price hits a certain resistance level that cannot be broken. After hitting this level, the price will bounce off it slightly, but then return back to test the level again. If the price bounces off of that level again, then you have a double top. If the second top cannot break the high of the first top, then this is a strong signal that a reversal is going to happen. A 'neckline' is drawn at the low between the two 'tops'. With a double top, you could think of placing your short (sell) entry order below the 'neckline' because you are expecting the trend to change downwards.

Your Next Steps

Before diving in, you could also prepare some more with an online class, I have one at (gcmsonline.info) or simply speaking with a trusted advisor. I will caution about using some of the online crypto forums. Most are without any sort of real supervision. Just a scan of several of the large ones available on the main social media networks and the answers provided to some of the questions from members are absolutely scary.

The past few months have shaken the confidence of many about the crypto markets, especially those who bought in December of 2017 to only see their accounts implode. I have met a few in class and I will share with you what I told them along with some charts: if in for the long term, take a deep breath and let things play themselves out. A lot of what we are seeing has been seen before in the crypto markets.

Bitcoin and cryptocurrencies have travelled far from the days of when they were mostly associated with criminals. Now there is both a broader and more positive public awareness. Bitcoin futures transactions are even cleared by top name Wall Street firms, something that not along ago would have been laughed at. For progress to continue as I have explained, there needs to be less hype, more relevant regulations, and greater security plus transparency from the exchanges. These suggestions I believe will secure that cryptocurrencies as an asset class moves beyond the early adopters phase.

Conclusion

Thank you for making it through to the end of *The Next Level Of Cryptocurrency Investing*. Let's hope it was informative and that it was able to provide you with some additional tools that will help you achieve your trading or investing goals. Your next move is to take action. Set up a demo account with your favorite trading provider and test your strategies until you achieve the results that you need to see before opening a live account.

My others books that have been proven to assist traders and investors are: *Technical Analysis for Forex Explained* and *Expert Advisor Programming for Beginners: Maximum MT4 Forex Profit Strategies*.

A preview paragraph from my next book: Crypto Algorithmic Trading Basics

Algorithmic (algos) trading is well-known for trading with the traditional asset classes like stocks, commodities and forex but not so much with cryptocurrencies.

For those unfamiliar with algos a quick refresher. An algo usually includes the following components: Entry signal, time frequency, size of the position, exit signal, and an evaluation benchmark to measure your success or lack of. Typically an algo will also include quite a bit of data mining which includes backtesting. The trap with backtesting is that some go too far back. In fact, this is one of the main reasons why many algos fail, the person or team behind it takes too long to go to market. The reality is market conditions change on a regular basis. For example, much of your backtest results, if doing it for forex, might become useless because of an unexpected interest rate change from a central bank.

Essential Bitcoin Crypto Vocabulary

Blockchain: Is a **public** record/ledger of Bitcoin transactions in chronological order. The blockchain is shared amongst all Bitcoin users. It is used to verify the permanence of Bitcoin transactions and to prevent double spending.

Block: Is a record in the blockchain that contains and confirms waiting transactions. Roughly every 10 minutes, on average, a new block including transactions is created to the blockchain through mining.

Genesis Block: This is the very first block that was created and the beginning of the blockchain.

Hash Rate: Is the measuring unit of the processing power of the Bitcoin network. The Bitcoin network must make intensive mathematical operations for security purposes. When the network reached a hash rate of 10 Th/s, it meant it could make 10 trillion calculations per second.

Mining: Is the process of making computer hardware do mathematical calculations for the Bitcoin network to confirm transactions and increase security. As a reward for their services, Bitcoin miners can collect transaction fees for the transactions they confirm, along with newly created bitcoins. Mining is specialized and competitive the rewards are divided up according to how much calculation is done.

Confirmation: Confirmation means that a transaction has been processed by the network and is highly unlikely to be reversed. Transactions receive a confirmation when they are included in a block and for each subsequent block. Even a single confirmation can be considered secure for low value transactions, although for larger amounts like 1,000 USD, it makes sense to wait for several more confirmations.

Double Spend: If a malicious user tries to spend their bitcoins to two different recipients at the same time, this is double spending. Bitcoin mining and the blockchain are there to create a consensus on the network about which of the two transactions will confirm and be considered valid.

Air Drop: Airdrop is the process where a cryptocurrency enterprise distributes cryptocurrency tokens to the wallets of some users free of charge. Airdrops are usually carried out by blockchain startups to bootstrap their projects.

Private Key: Is a secret piece of data that proves your right to spend bitcoins from a specific wallet through a cryptographic signature. Your private key(s) are stored in your computer if you use a software wallet; they are stored on some remote servers if you use a web wallet. Private keys must never be revealed as they allow you to spend bitcoins for their respective Bitcoin wallet.

Signature: A cryptographic signature is a mathematical mechanism that allows someone to prove ownership. In the case of Bitcoin, a Bitcoin wallet and its private key(s) are linked by mathematical magic. When your Bitcoin software signs a transaction with the appropriate private key, the whole network can see that the signature matches the bitcoins being spent. However, there is no way for the world to guess your private key to steal your bitcoins.

Wallet: A Bitcoin wallet is loosely the equivalent of a physical wallet on the Bitcoin network. The wallet actually contains your private key(s) which allow you to spend the bitcoins allocated to it in the blockchain. Each Bitcoin wallet can show you the total balance of all bitcoins it controls and lets you pay an amount to a specific person.

Cold Storage: This is the process of moving your bitcoins to an offline wallet. The benefit of this is that no one can hack into your computer and steal your private keys if your computer is not connected to a network. Bitcoins will need to be brought back out of cold storage to be spent or transferred again.

Fungibility: Is the property of a good or a commodity whose individual units are interchangeable. For example, since one kilo of pure gold is equivalent to any other kilo of pure gold, whether in the form of coins or in other states, gold is fungible. Other fungible commodities include, crude oil, shares, bonds, currencies. A diamond is not since each is unique.

Address: A Bitcoin address is a unique string of 27-34 alphanumeric characters. An address can be created freely with the use of a wallet and always starts with a 1 or a 3.

Alternate Currencies (altcoins): The many different alternative currencies that have sprung up based off the idea and/or basic code of Bitcoin. A few of the more notable ones are Litecoin, IOTA, and Ripple.

Fork: A "fork" is a change to the software of a digital currency that creates two separate versions of the blockchain with a shared history. Forks can be temporary or they can be a permanent split in the network creating two separate versions of the blockchain. When this happens, two different digital currencies are also created.

DDOS: Short for 'Distributed Denial of Service'. A well-timed DDoS attack at exchanges during volatile movements may be devastating as traders will not be able to execute any order manually and will be at the mercy of their pre-set orders.

ERC20: A technical standard used for smart contracts on the Ethereum blockchain for implementing tokens. *ERC* stands for *Ethereum Request for Comment*, and *20* is the number that was assigned to this request.

ERC20 defines a common list of rules for Ethereum tokens to follow within the larger Ethereum ecosystem, allowing developers to accurately predict interaction between tokens.

Profile of The Author

Wayne Walker is the director of a global capital markets education and consulting firm (gcmsonline.info). He has several years experience in leading and coaching teams of Investment Advisors and has managed top performing teams in the Private Client Group based on Bench Mark Earnings (BME).